MLM for MOM

WHY NETWORK MARKETING IS A NATURAL FIT FOR MOTHERS

Amy Starr Allen

BALBOA.
PRESS
A DIVISION OF HAY HOUSE

Balboa Press books may be ordered through booksellers or by contacting:

Balboa Press
A Division of Hay House
1663 Liberty Drive
Bloomington, IN 47403
www.balboapress.com
1-(877) 407-4847

Because of the dynamic nature of the Internet, any web addresses or links contained in this book may have changed since publication and may no longer be valid. The views expressed in this work are solely those of the author and do not necessarily reflect the views of the publisher, and the publisher hereby disclaims any responsibility for them.

The author of this book does not dispense medical advice or prescribe the use of any technique as a form of treatment for physical, emotional, or medical problems without the advice of a physician, either directly or indirectly. The intent of the author is only to offer information of a general nature to help you in your quest for emotional and spiritual well-being. In the event you use any of the information in this book for yourself, which is your constitutional right, the author and the publisher assume no responsibility for your actions.

Any people depicted in stock imagery provided by Thinkstock are models, and such images are being used for illustrative purposes only.
Certain stock imagery © Thinkstock.

Printed in the United States of America

ISBN 978-1-4525-3924-9 (sc)
ISBN 978-1-4525-3925-6 (ebk)

Balboa Press rev. date: 10/03/2011

TABLE OF CONTENTS

DEDICATION

This book is dedicated to the loving memory of my dear friend Suzi Granger who came into my life thanks to the Network Marketing industry. Suzi was a gigantic light in my life and she was a pure example of, and a stand for, the amazing community we have access to here.

You have truly left a legacy for all of us, Suzi, and I will always hold you fondly in my heart.

Special thanks:

To my beautiful daughters, Olivia and Ava, who motivate me to be the best I can be every day in every aspect of my life.

To my loving father, my awesome stepmother, and my incredible brother, Lionel, for always believing in me and supporting me in all of the wild and sometimes crazy ventures I tend to undertake.

To David McLaughlin, Annie Schellenberg, Christa Way, and Michael Jude who have stood by my side for the entire 8 years I've been in this industry and who continue to call me forward into my magnificence every single day.

To Wayne & Gerri Hillman (the wonderful founders of the company I'm involved with), for your vision, your support, and your undying love for all of us.

To Marjorie Lynn and Alex Theis for standing with me and believing in me as we move forward into the vision of empowering mothers everywhere and making a significant impact on the world.

To the millions of mothers on the planet who inspire me on a daily basis. It is because of you that this book was written and that I am given the profound honor of living my true passion every single day.

PREFACE

It is because of my deep passion for the Network Marketing industry and what it has provided for myself and my daughters that I was moved to write *MLM for MOM*. My goal is to help get this message out to mothers everywhere, to show why the Network Marketing industry truly is a natural fit for mothers, and to help make this world a little bit better for my having been here.

There are 4 other amazing mothers who have contributed chapters to *MLM for MOM*. The message received from each of these women is unique, educational, and profound. I am humbled and it is a great honor and privilege to be able to feature each of these women in *MLM for MOM*.

My sincere thanks to Nicole S. Cooper, Chante Epps-McDonald, Cindy Lapp, and Ali Alvarez. Your contribution to *MLM for MOM* is extraordinary, and I am in deep gratitude.

INTRODUCTION

My name is Amy Starr Allen and I'm a single mom. I've been involved in the Network Marketing industry for over 8 years, and could not be more passionate about what this industry provides for people, particularly mothers.

When I was first introduced to the company I'm with and the Network Marketing industry, I was working full-time in corporate America. I was working in the music industry and, being a singer-songwriter myself, this felt like the ideal job for me (other than the fact, of course, that I was barely making enough to get by and I had no time to do the things I really wanted to do with my life!).

When I was introduced to the concept of Network Marketing, I immediately liked the idea of it and began to invest a small amount of my non-working hours into building the business on the side. Eventually, I got married, left the music industry, and started to pursue other types of entrepreneurial careers such as real estate and personal training. I continued to chip away at my Network Marketing business in the midst of everything else I was doing, and was slowly but surely creating a small residual income that I could count on month after month, regardless of how much time I spent on my business in any given month.

Then I got pregnant. About 6 months into my pregnancy as I thought about bringing a child into the world, I got VERY CLEAR that I didn't want to continue working full-time. I didn't want to be away from my child for that many hours each week.

What I realized was that, although I really loved real estate and personal training (two things that I happen to be very passionate about), both of these careers required trading hours for dollars which meant:

1. I had to work a lot to make a decent income and
2. No matter how many hours I worked, there was a limit to how much I could earn (there are only so many hours in the day, after all).

Then it hit me. As I was sitting in the international convention for my Network Marketing company, watching all kinds of people (most of which had been involved in the company a lot less time than I had) walk across the stage receiving awards for their accomplishments, I got it. I realized that I loved what I was doing, I just wasn't spending very much time doing it. I also realized it was the *only* source of income that I had that did *not* require trading hours for dollars (in this business I was creating residual income, which meant that I could do the work once and continue to get paid on it month after month).

In that moment I knew that if I really got committed to my business, I could actually create a SIGNIFICANT residual income, and then I wouldn't have to keep trading hours for dollars and I could spend a lot more time with my daughter. I also knew that out of all of the things I was doing, this business gave me the biggest opportunity to make a *profound* difference for people (real estate sales and personal training did make a difference, but this was an opportunity to help people with their time freedom, their financial freedom, and their health all at once . . . what a gift!).

From that point forward, I committed to really succeeding in Network Marketing. Since then I had another child, got a divorce, and replaced my other sources of income with my residual check from my Network Marketing business, so that I can now do this business full-time.

THE DIVORCE

What happened during the process of my divorce is something that has had a significant impact on me, my children, and my passion for this business and this industry. Although I started writing this book while I was married, the course of events that have taken place since then have fueled my fire for this business in such a big way that I feel it's important I share them with you. In all probability, the chances that *you* are a mother (since you're reading this book) are pretty high, and this information might make a difference for you.

Five short weeks after my second daughter was born (while I was still recovering from childbirth), my husband and I split up, very abruptly. I don't need to go into the details, I'll just say that I became a single mom COMPLETELY in that instant, something that I was in no way prepared for.

Not only was this a very emotional time for me and my children (as anyone who has been through a divorce can certainly relate to), but there was a lot to do. I had to find another place to live, I had to move, I had to find a counselor for my 3-year-old who was devastated, I had to hire a lawyer, and on and on . . . you get the picture. And now, for the first time since my kids had been born, it was all up to me. I no longer had a partner to help hold down the fort or to help out with *anything*.

During this time, my business took a back seat to everything else I had going on, to say the least. I ended up completely checking out of my business due to necessity, for four full months.

Here's the beautiful thing . . . during those four months, my monthly residual checks continued to show up in my mailbox. And they were enough to support my family so that I didn't have to go out and get a job. And here's the thing that you really need to understand: During those four crazy months, I didn't work, *at all*.

I didn't work one bit and I got paid anyway. Wow, what a concept.

I mean, I knew I was in the business of residual income, and was certainly passionate about what that could provide for people, but never before had I actually put it to the test and stopped working completely while the checks continued to roll in.

During the course of these four months there was an event going on for my company and the owners of the company were in town. I stopped by the event for a few minutes with my baby to say hello, and as soon as I saw the owners of my company my eyes welled up with tears. All I could say to them was, "Thank you. Thank you so much for this amazing opportunity. I don't even know what I would have done otherwise, this is such an incredible gift . . . thank you!" And I cried.

Once things settled down a bit and I was ready to jump into my business again, I did with a new-found passion. I had (and still have) a whole new appreciation for the industry that I'm involved with and what it provides for people and families.

So now more than ever I feel compelled to get the word out. I truly believe that the pain that I suffered was a catalyst to move me closer to my purpose. I truly believe that one of my biggest jobs while I'm here on this earth is to educate people about the choices that they have and opportunities that they wouldn't have known existed. And this industry now holds, and will always hold, a really special place in my heart.

GLOSSARY

There are several terms we use when referring to the Network Marketing industry. The terms are used interchangeably throughout this book, so I wanted to go ahead and define them for you.

Network Marketing—Also known as relationship marketing, is a marketing strategy that compensates independent unsalaried sales people referred to as distributors (or associates, independent business owners, sales consultants, consultants, independent agents, etc.)

MLM—Multi-Level Marketing, another name for Network Marketing

Other terms used to describe our industry:

Referral Marketing

Direct Sales

Residual Income—Income that continues to come in after you stop working. Often times in the Network Marketing industry, we do the work once and continue to get paid on it month after month, year after year. This income is generated due to the loyalty of our customers who continue to order products (usually through an automatic shipment that requires no extra work on the distributor's part) month after month. It is residual income that allows people in the Network Marketing industry to get paid whether they work or not, and it is this type of income that creates time freedom.

Residual income is a great way to fund your retirement, and in many instances (depending on which company you join in the Network Marketing industry), it is a stream of income that can be willed to your children or the charity of your choice.

CHAPTER 1

MOTHERS MAKE GREAT LEADERS

Mother love is the fuel that enables a normal human being to do the impossible. ~Marion C. Garretty

It's no wonder so many mothers are successful at this type of business. A friend of mine recently said to me, "You are a force to be dealt with." What's funny about this is that not-too-many years ago, people didn't even know what a woman (let alone *mother*) entrepreneur was. And, according to a White House task force, in the corporate world, women earn just 76 cents for every dollar that men earn, which is another reason so many of us are seeking entrepreneurial opportunities.

Mothers have a lot of great attributes that lend to them being successful in this industry. Let's look at some of the qualities that many mothers possess that contribute to their success.

MOTHERS ARE MULTI-TASKERS

Any mother could perform the jobs of several air traffic controllers with ease. ~Lisa Alther

I don't think I've ever met a mother that wasn't capable of accomplishing a handful of tasks simultaneously. It's part of the deal, really. When you have children, you must learn to juggle. It's the only way to get anything done. This quality is very beneficial once a woman (or anyone) starts a Network Marketing business.

The nice thing about our industry is that it definitely allows for a great deal of flexibility. People can work according to their own schedules, and many people work their MLM business in conjunction with a separate full-time job. That being said, it also takes some discipline to work this business into our already chaotic lives. This is where being a mother comes in handy. We're already used to doing this . . . it's called multi-tasking.

Have you ever heard the saying, "If you need something done, give it to a busy person"? In other words, don't look for someone who has nothing going on in their life (this is usually a sure sign of laziness) and expect them to jump up and suddenly start accomplishing all kinds of things. A busy person, on the other hand, knows she can get it done, as she has proven this to herself time and time again.

I know I can speak from experience here. I'm one of those people who seems to always have a ton going on, an absolutely full schedule, and when someone calls and says, "Can you help us organize x for the next 3 months and take on being in charge of z?" I almost always respond with, "Yes! I'd be happy to!" I mean, what's one more thing on my plate anyway? Not a big deal.

The beautiful thing about many Network Marketing businesses is that they simply don't take up that much time. We can certainly find the time to manage them into our schedules if we really want to make it work (where there's a will, there's a way).

Mothers Are Very Nurturing

Sweater, n.: garment worn by child when its mother is feeling chilly.
~Ambrose Bierce

Caring for others is another quality that seems to come naturally for most mothers. It, once again, just goes along with the game. If you want to raise kids, you have to care for them, right?

Network Marketing is a business built on relationships. We build relationships, and then we nurture those relationships. The easiest way to succeed in this industry is to focus on other people. If you focus on others and their dreams and helping them to succeed, there's no way you can't succeed yourself! And usually, depending on the compensation plan within the company you choose, it only takes bringing on a few people and helping them to succeed to take you all the way to the top where you will be earning a substantial income.

What's great about this is that this is what we love to do anyway (and what we're already really good at). We want to make a difference for people, to nurture them, and to help them succeed. What career could be more fun, or more fulfilling? And it just comes naturally for so many of us. (Again, it's no wonder there are so many leaders in our industry who are mothers).

Mothers Are Great Communicators

The best conversations with mothers always take place in silence, when only the heart speaks. ~Carrie Latet

Communication is certainly a key to our success in this industry. Every aspect of this business requires a great deal of communicating, and we need to be able to communicate effectively to get the job done.

Communication is also a key to success when it comes to parenting. There are tricks to becoming an effective communicator in order to raise great children. It's essential for us to master this skill in our relationships with our children in order to get the job done well. And effective communication is also one of the key pieces to becoming a leader in the Network Marketing industry.

Point made? Mothers make great leaders because they are already multi-taskers, nurturers and great communicators (among about a million other things), which makes them prime candidates to succeed in the Network Marketing industry.

CHAPTER 2

CHANTE EPPS-MCDONALD

www.ChanteEpps.com

This industry and being an entrepreneur and just Network Marketing in general is helping me to develop into everything that I know I'm supposed to be. ~ Chante Epps

I got started in the Network Marketing industry in 2010. I was actually introduced to the industry in 2009, so it just took me a while to get started. I have a 9-year-old and a 5-year-old, both boys.

I do this business full time. It became an option for me when I got laid off in 2009. I was trying to find a job and it just wasn't happening, so I decided to take advantage of what Network Marketing had to offer.

Before getting started in this industry, I was a legal secretary at a law firm. I was looking for ways to start my own business, as I knew I wanted to own my own business, I just didn't know what I wanted to do. This was prior to me getting laid off, but there were massive layoffs happening in my company and I knew I needed to start thinking about what else I could do, just in case this was to happen to me.

I considered opening a traditional Brick & Mortar store, but I knew I didn't want to take out loans for tens of thousands or hundreds of thousands of dollars just to get a business started.

I started doing some research on the internet to find out what some of my options were, and that's when a family member introduced me to Network Marketing.

I was definitely quite skeptical about it at first. I knew there was money to be made, I just didn't really understand how. And I wasn't sure which opportunities were legitimate because there were so many scams out there.

This industry has been a real blessing for me. When I lost my job (this was the second time I had been laid off), I decided I was through with corporate America. I decided I needed to do something so that I would never have to set foot in a corporate office again.

Network Marketing has provided time freedom for me.

When I was working a corporate job, I was always at the office and if I wanted to take the day off to participate in an activity with my children, I would always get this awkward silence over the phone. The same would happen if I had to call in because my children were sick. I'm sure this is a lot of moms' experience. Nobody ever understood.

I hated that feeling. I hated that feeling of having to compromise my life as a mother and being there for my children for corporate America. I seriously hated it with a passion.

Now I look at me being laid off as an answer to my prayers.

I would literally pray about that. I wanted to be able to spend time with my family. I felt stressed out from working all the time and I didn't have time to do the things I wanted to do with my family. The weekends became very rushed because I was trying to fit in all my household duties as a mom and as a wife in addition to having time to spend with my children, all in just 2 days on the weekend. I always felt so rushed.

Now I'm able to attend my children's functions at school, I'm able to be a chaperone on their trips, and I really enjoy it. It has opened my eyes as to where I need to be. I need to be more involved with my children and more involved in their school activities.

And I'm finding that my children are flourishing as well.

My 5-year-old plays the violin and he is AWESOME. His music teacher goes on and on about him, and I know that one of the main reasons is because I've been able to take him to violin lessons, something I wouldn't have been able to do if I still had a job.

Lots of great opportunities are opening up for my kids at school. I find myself much more devoted to their studies, and I truly feel that this was what was needed for me as a mom to be able to help my kids in school and to be able to be there for them emotionally and physically.

This industry has also allowed my children to be opened up to entrepreneurship. They are heavily involved in what I do and they're excited about seeing me do my business. They love seeing me get all of my calls, and they know the names of other marketers and of my mentors.

I was not exposed to this type of industry when I was younger. And I love that my children are in the presence of people who are making six and seven figures. They see me being comfortable and at home around extremely successful people, and they even understand and get excited about the different trips that I take to participate in different industry and company events.

I've even heard my son say, "I want my own business when I grow up." That just helps me know that I'm on the right path.

I was always taught something different, and I feel like my children are getting a head start because they get to see me do this and live it out in front of them.

I absolutely recommend this industry for mothers. Even if they start off part time and just start building something on the side to help supplement their income, I cannot recommend it more highly. It's been worth every dime I've spent and it just means so much to be able to spend more time with my children.

And there's no feeling like seeing my children excited because I get to participate in their school functions now. When I was at work, I couldn't do that.

This industry and being an entrepreneur and just network marketing in general is helping me to develop into everything that I know I'm supposed to be.

It's helping me face my fears, it's helping me deal with issues that need to be dealt with in order for me to be successful, and it's helping me overcome my insecurities. Being an entrepreneur is helping me to become a stronger person and teaching me to face things head on.

It's also inspiring me to help others. When I first got started in this industry, it was all about the money. But now when I see the people's lives that I'm impacting, when I hear the passion in their voices, when I hear how excited they are to talk to me and to hear what I have to share with them, it does something to me. There's no feeling like it.

I'm also really excited about what's to come, and I'm just embracing the process!

CHAPTER 3

Basics About the Network Marketing Industry

The best time to plant a tree was 20 years ago. The next best time is now. ~ Chinese Proverb

In 1975 the Federal Trade Commission accused and sued Amway Corporation for operating as an illegal pyramid. After four years of litigation the court ruled that Amway's multi-level-marketing program was a legitimate business and not a pyramid scheme.

In 1979, the Network Marketing industry was proven a legal form of distributing goods and services by the U.S. Federal Government. This was known as the 'Amway Decision' and this event paved the way for the emergence of the hugely successful Network Marketing industry.

The direct selling industry has been growing like wildfire ever since. According to the World Federation of Direct Selling Associations, direct selling worldwide accounted for more than $111 billion in sales and employed more than 67 million independent sales representatives in 2007.

In addition, the MLM business model has proven itself highly effective at distributing products and services to consumers based on the same benchmarks used by Wall Street. This form of distribution is one of the most ethical ways of doing business. There is no 'middle man' involved and no high-paid celebrities advertising products. Network Marketing companies simply pay commissions to independent distributors who get the word out about their products and services.

In many companies, the commission payout is extremely generous and makes it relatively easy for people to create a full-time income. These companies can afford these generous payouts due to the fact that they do not have to share their profits with middle men (retail stores) or maintain a high advertising budget.

As we move into the age of the entrepreneur, more and more people are wanting to (and starting to) go into business for themselves. There are huge tax incentives for starting a home-based business, and with the uncertainty as far as job stability in today's economy, people are looking for more secure ways to make a living.

The Network Marketing industry allows people to go into business for themselves with very little start-up costs, low or no overhead, no employees, and an extremely flexible schedule. There is also, in many cases, unlimited earning potential, so people can not only make a living, they can make a fortune . . . all while having the freedom to spend more time with their families and do the things they enjoy in life.

COMPETITIVE VS. COOPERATIVE

Competition has been shown to be useful up to a certain point and no further, but cooperation, which is the thing we must strive for today, begins where competition leaves off. ~ Franklin D. Roosevelt

One of the things I love most about the way we do business in this industry is the fact that we use a cooperative business model rather than a competitive one like they use in corporate America. Network Marketing is actually one of the most ethical ways of doing business, and it's largely due to this business model.

The competitive business model, as used in corporate America, is much more common. In this model, if someone wants to advance in the company they literally have to wait for someone to quit, die, or retire. It causes the workplace to become very cut-throat and competitive. I mean, you wouldn't want to share all of your success secrets with a business associate and help them to be more successful only to run the risk of them getting the promotion instead of you, would you? Of course not!

It ends up becoming an "every man for himself" kind of environment, and often times this leads to a lack of trust, etc. It's hard to really befriend someone when your consistently competing with them, isn't it?

Now let's look at the cooperative business model that's used in a lot of Network Marketing companies. In this model, we get paid on the efforts of other people. Therefore, it's in our best interest to help others succeed.

When I sponsor someone into my business, I want them to be as successful as possible. I am going to get paid for all of their efforts and successes, and I am willing to do everything I can to assure that they are successful. I will provide coaching and training for free, and I will make myself totally available for this person. Not only that, but in this model it's a level playing field. This means that there's room for all of us at the top. The companies in the Network Marketing industry would love it if we all were constantly advancing in rank, therefore there's no competition.

Let's compare the two business models for a moment. The competitive model, like corporate America, is shaped like a pyramid. The CEO is at the top of the triangle, under him are the VP's, then the middle management, etc. all the way down to the minimum wage employees who are sweeping the floor. In this model, the people at the top got there either due to their education, experience, or relationship with someone they know at the top. There's absolutely no chance for the janitor way down at the bottom of the pyramid to ever make his way into one of the VP slots. It's highly unlikely this would ever happen within the political structure of this business model.

Competitive Business Model

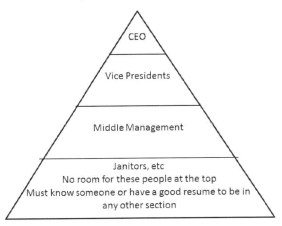

In the cooperative model on the other hand, EVERYONE comes in at the bottom. It doesn't matter what race or religion you have or what kind of degree you hold. We advance in rank based on our performance alone, and those who produce the most get paid the most. It's a completely level playing field, totally fair and ethical. Everyone has the same chance at succeeding. Actually, sometimes the ones we least expect are the ones who become the most successful. It's all about action and results, not education. As a matter of fact, because of the cooperative nature of this model, the education needed is provided by the person or team that sponsors a new person, happily and for free.

Cooperative Business Model

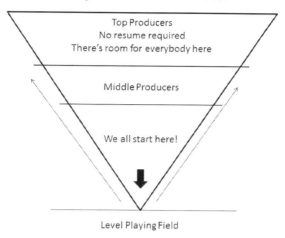

Top Producers
No resume required
There's room for everybody here

Middle Producers

We all start here!

Level Playing Field

It's because of the way we do business in this industry that we are able to form these tight knit communities of people that are really there for each other through thick and thin. We are continuously helping each other rather than competing with each other, and the types of friendships that are formed here are deep and lasting.

Rather than the "every man for himself" environment, we work in a "one for all and all for one" environment, being of service to each other and supporting each other. Having experienced both myself, I'd choose the cooperative model over the competitive one any day . . . it's really a lot more fun.

CHAPTER 4

BEING THE FAMILY BREADWINNER

I make an active effort to remain a positive role model to kids. They need people to show them there's another way. ~M.C. Hammer

There's never been a better time to go into business for ourselves. Not long ago, people who started their own businesses were not given the same respect as heads of corporations, doctors, lawyers, etc. even though many of them made millions. But now these same entrepreneurs are well respected and seen as trendsetters.

There are many reasons that women are, much more regularly, going out on their own. For one, many women have experienced barriers to advancement in the corporate world, having a cap on the amount of income they can make.

Another major reason many women are leaving the corporate world is for more flexibility. We want to be able to choose when we work, and have the flexibility to spend more time with our children.

And then, of course, there's our desire to be creative and to think outside the box. It's very difficult to accomplish either of these things in the corporate world.

If you are a productive person, *you will probably be very intrigued by what the Network Marketing industry offers.* In this industry, you are able to create a pay raise any time you want, and there is no limit to how much money you can make.

I could go on and on about the many reasons women are leaving the workplace to branch off on their own. But now let's just look at some of the benefits of starting a business in the Network Marketing industry.

- You can have a business of your own
- You can work from home
- It usually requires very little start-up cost
- It doesn't require having any employees
- You have unlimited earning potential
- You can create a passive residual income
- You have a team of people who will train and support you
- You make your own schedule and work as much or as little as you want
- You get to choose who you work with and who you spend your time with
- You get to work cooperatively with associates instead of competing with them

Basically, we're at a time in history where traditional business offers very little security. The Network Marketing industry allows individuals, by investing a small sum of money, to create a great amount of personal and financial freedom. This is an industry where, with consistent effort, it is possible to succeed in a reasonable amount of time starting with next to nothing. And this can all be done from home!

Women, once again, are very good at forming meaningful relationships. And that's really what's at the core of this business. The most successful people in our industry are often the ones that are really good at building strong relationships with the people that join them in their businesses. Exhibiting leadership skills and having a big heart and strong desire to help others is what will attract people to want to work with you in this industry. And, once again, most mothers possess all of these qualities.

Now I want to touch on some of the benefits of being involved in this amazing industry and what's possible when you become the family breadwinner.

Retiring Your Husband

Are you married to someone who works so much that he isn't able to spend much time with the family? Does your husband dislike his job or the time commitment involved?

Do you know anyone else whose family situation looks something like this?

One of the wonderful things about the Network Marketing industry is that there is no limit on the amount of money that can be earned. Many women in our industry have set goals to be able to retire their husbands from their current employment situation, and many women in our industry have actually achieved this.

There is no greater gift than having a large enough residual income to be able to tell your husband, "Honey, you can quit your job now. My income is more than enough to support our family."

Being in Business With Your Husband

Another benefit of this industry is that you can be in business with your spouse and build your business together as a team.

We have seen countless couples who have achieved great success working together, not to mention how much fun they have working together as a team and building their fortunes and their future together.

And, when the kids are old enough, you can get them involved, too! My oldest daughter is only 6, but she loves being involved in any way she can. She helps me put stamps on envelopes and other little tasks. And she loves being involved in the community with all of the other kids she gets to spend time with when we have company and industry gatherings.

Being A Positive Role Model For Your Children

Being the family breadwinner provides much more than just a significant income for our children. When our kids see us making a difference in the world and working as an entrepreneur to provide lots of vacations and a great lifestyle for them, it teaches them that this is a possibility for them as well.

When I was growing up (and I know this is true for many people), I wasn't aware that an option like this was available. All I knew was that I needed to get good grades so that I could grow up and get a good job working for someone else (building their fortune instead of my own).

One of the things I love the most about what I'm doing now is that I'm teaching my children, by example, that they have choices. I'm teaching them that time freedom and financial freedom are possibilities for them as well, and that they can grow up and find something that they truly love to do and get paid really well to do it.

I'm also showing them that it is possible for a parent to never miss a beat in their kids' lives. Since I make my own schedule, I'm able to be very active in my daughters' lives and I never miss an important event. I even show up at the school at lunchtime on some days and eat lunch in the cafeteria with my daughter (she LOVES that)! I'm also able to volunteer in the classroom and chaperone field trips, etc.

Being a single parent, this is rare. Most single parents who are also the family breadwinner are off working all of the time and missing out on much of their children's lives.

As we all know, our children grow up way too fast, and I am so unbelievably grateful to be able to be an active part of my children's lives every day.

BEING A ROLE MODEL FOR SOCIETY

When we become the family breadwinner, we not only become a positive role model for our children, but we become a positive role model for society as well.

What a powerful statement we get to make when we retire our husbands or demonstrate the lifestyle freedom that's available through our industry.

Unfortunately, there are still many people in the world who are working at jobs they dislike and are completely unaware that an option like this exists. When we achieve success for ourselves, we also teach others that it's possible, and we give others permission to go after their dreams as well.

This, in my opinion, is a huge contribution to society.

CHAPTER 5

COMMUNITY

Friends can help each other. A true friend is someone who lets you have total freedom to be yourself—and especially to feel. Or, not feel. Whatever you happen to be feeling at the moment is fine with them. That's what real love amounts to—letting a person be what he really is. ~Jim Morrison

Network Marketing is a wonderful social activity. This industry is a great place to meet people and have fun. There are business meetings, training meetings, cruises, potlucks, and retreats where you can meet lots of new like-minded friends.

At Network Marketing events, it's easy to get involved in great conversations about business or personal growth. I know many people who have found their spouses in this industry because there are so many people and so many events where you can go and be around like-minded people.

Every 12-18 months most Network Marketing companies hold national or international conventions where people meet from all over the world. I have met some of my closest friends from all over the world at my company's international convention that takes place every year.

As you've probably heard me mention before, in my opinion, the community aspect of this business is one of the biggest benefits that this industry has to offer. The relationships formed out of this business are invaluable, and they're certainly not the typical "when the going's good" surface-type relationships.

We celebrate our victories together (often on a daily basis) and support (and coach) each other during discouraging times. We're also called on to lead by example which really keeps us on our toes. We get to know each other on a very intimate level, and call out the magnificence in each other. The relationships formed here are solid. They're the type where, for example, I know if I needed to, I could call any of my business partners in the middle of the night and they would be there for me with whatever I needed without batting an eyelash. It's what the founder of my company likes to call "love-sharing".

SUZI'S MARK ON THE WORLD

If you go looking for a friend, you're going to find they're very scarce.
If you go out to be a friend, you'll find them everywhere. ~Zig Ziglar

I recently went to a memorial service for a dear friend that passed away. Her name is Suzi, and she's someone that I met years ago at the international convention for my Network Marketing company. She had, just prior to that convention, moved here from Australia to marry a man she met on the internet and didn't know many people. We sat on the beach together in San Diego during the breaks and discovered we had a lot in common. We became fast friends and had remained very close ever since.

The service for Suzi was beautiful, absolutely amazing. There was an open forum where anyone who wanted to could get up and speak about their fond memories of Suzi and many beautiful rituals were performed. The thing that blew my mind, though, more than anything else about the service was the sense of community. I was amazed by the number of incredible people that were there and the vast, high quality community that Suzi had created in the 5 short years that she'd been living in the states.

I looked around and saw a lot of people from my company, and I got really present to the most powerful and wonderful benefit that comes out of doing a business like this: community.

My Community

The people in this community have become some of my best friends over the last 8 years that I've been doing this business. They are extraordinary people. They are people that are up to something, people that are creating residual income and making a difference in the world, people that are committed to health, people that are raising money for charities and starting foundations, people that really take care of each other.

I think about some of the hard times I've endured in the past 8 years and how the people from this community were there to support me every step of the way. I think about the times when I questioned whether this type of business was going to work for me, and that what kept me in it was the irreplaceable community I had created *because* of this business.

We are so incredibly fortunate to have the opportunity to be involved in a business like this, that not only provides unlimited earning potential and residual income, but a chance to be a part of a meaningful, extraordinary community.

Playing Together

Since we're all creating wealth and time freedom together, it is this community that we get to play with, travel with, celebrate with, and have fun with as well.

How many times have you tried to plan a vacation, a weekend, or even just a concert or an event with someone who said, "I'd love to, but I have to work."

In this industry, since we're all up to creating wealth and time freedom, we get to vacation together, go on adventures together, and spend lots of quality time together. And the beautiful thing about this is that we also get to *choose* who we work with. So while we're choosing who we want to work with, we can also be thinking about who we want to play with and travel with!

CHAPTER 6

Nicole S. Cooper

www.TheMailboxMoneyBlog.com

> *As a mother we're faced with all kinds of challenges, and when we get around our network marketing community, it's like a breath of fresh air. ~ Nicole S. Cooper*

I've been in the Network Marketing industry on and off for about 15 years. I started in 1996. I have one child, a 3-year-old daughter, Chloe.

I've been a full-time Network Marketer for many years, and just recently started implementing another entrepreneurial business. Before starting a Network Marketing business, I had a career in Real Estate.

As a mother, this industry gives you freedom, and it also gives your child exposure to entrepreneurship. We all obviously want to be able to be home to take care of our children. What this industry has done for me is it's given me control. It allows me to be home when I need to be, to take Chloe to the doctor or gymnastics or any other form of outlet. This industry allows me the freedom to be able to do all of these things rather than having to go to a job and be restricted.

What this industry has provided for Chloe is access to her mom whenever she needs it. Sometimes she has to share because I do work from home and my attention can't always be on her, but she knows that she always has access to her mom.

Network Marketing is great for moms because it gives them self-esteem and a whole bunch of other benefits that are often not mentioned when they're being exposed to this type of business opportunity.

This industry helps to reshape the mindset that women have to push their goals and dreams aside, and teaches them how to embrace their dreams and goals.

Network Marketing teaches people how to pursue their dreams and gives them the finances to be able to pursue them.

This industry also provides you with the network of people who will give you the support that you need.

The thing about moms is that we are so selfless. We don't think about ourselves, we think about everybody else. The truth is that we need a team, we need support, we need cheerleaders. Being in the Network Marketing industry actually gives you access to that support and it surrounds you with people who will help you reach your goals.

As a mother we're faced with all kinds of challenges, and when we get around our network marketing community, it's like a breath of fresh air. When you don't show up, people miss you, people are always checking on you, and amazing relationships are developed. It's just a good support system for women to help them remember that they need to be on their to-do list as well.

I think it's important for people to think about the one cause they have in life.

All of us have a purpose. All of us have things that we dream of doing and desire to do, but we often feel restricted because of a lack of resources, a lack of time, a lack of money, or a lack of support. To me, Network Marketing is a great starting point for you if you don't know where you should be going, if you haven't discovered your cause. It helps you to establish and discover your cause. It helps you to determine where you should be focusing your energy and some of the things that you should really be pursuing that would add more purpose and value to your life.

I really encourage people to pursue this industry so that they can explore who they really are and determine some of the things that they really want to do in life, so that they don't push their goals and dreams aside and think that they are too old or it's too late, or it's too far-fetched or too impossible.

These benefits of Network Marketing are very rarely promoted. These are the kinds of things that people need to know exist within our industry. This industry is definitely not just about selling a product.

CHAPTER 7

DOING WHAT YOU LOVE

Choose a job you love, and you will never have to work a day in your life. ~ Confucius

How many people can honestly say that they love what they do, especially when they are working for someone else, building someone else's dreams and having a cap on how much income they can earn (not to mention have someone else dictate when they get to take time off, how many hours they work, etc.)?

It's great to be able to spend my time the way I want to. I get to get up (without an alarm clock), have breakfast with my kids, and work according to my own schedule. I believe there are millions of people in the world who would love to do what I do.

The relationships that have come out of my doing this business are extremely rewarding. As I've mentioned, I've literally made some of the best friends in my life by doing this business.

It's great because there's no separation between work and pleasure like there was in the corporate world. This business is really about forming relationships with people and helping them fulfill on their dreams, while forming deep partnerships along the way. Our success is actually dependent on how many people we help become successful. Not to mention we get to experience the joy of sharing a product with people that has the potential to change their lives. It doesn't get any more fun (or fulfilling) than that!

The key to succeeding in this industry is to find something (a company and a product) that you can truly get passionate about. When you find something you love to do, it won't even feel like 'work'. And the beauty of this ever-growing industry is that there are thousands of companies to choose from. (I will go into more detail about choosing a company in the next chapter).

ACHIEVE YOUR OTHER DREAMS

Many people have dreams that they fail to acknowledge due to "not enough time" or "not enough money". It may be travel, music, art, dancing, flying, diving, golf . . . the list is literally endless.

One of the benefits of this industry is that it allows us access to residual income (we do the work once and continue to get paid for it month after month) which creates time freedom in our lives. And, once we have time freedom, we can start to pursue the things we are truly passionate about in our lives (art, music, travel or whatever it may be).

This book is a perfect example of this. I've always wanted to write a book and I know that if I was still working a full-time job on top of being a single mother, the likelihood that I would have been able to find time to write this book is slim to none. It's only because of residual income and time freedom that I was able to pull it off. And, thanks to residual income, I actually got paid while I was writing the book.

LIVE WHERE YOU WANT

In this industry, not only do we get to find a company and a product that we can get passionate about and do what we love, but we get to live wherever we want as well.

We get to exit the "rat race" lifestyle and stop commuting, forever. In the Network Marketing industry, we get to work from home. As long as you have a phone, you can literally work from anywhere, and therefore live anywhere you'd like.

What if I already love what I do?

Maybe you have a career that you love. Maybe you're a doctor or a massage therapist or a beautician and you love your work and the fact that you get to make a difference for people on a regular basis.

But, maybe you feel somewhat trapped because you have to go to work in order to be able to pay the bills, and if you stop working you stop getting paid.

What's great about this industry is that people can work at their MLM business part-time until they earn enough income to quit their full-time job (if they desire to do so). For those that don't want to quit their current profession, they can cut back on their hours and remove the stress of working because they have to. And cutting back on our hours, again, allows us the time freedom to pursue some of our other passions in life.

CHAPTER 8

CHOOSING THE RIGHT COMPANY

Time is the friend of the wonderful company, the enemy of the mediocre.
~Warren Buffett

The key to success in this industry, is finding a company and a product that you can get truly passionate about. As I spoke about in the last chapter, when you love what you do, it doesn't even feel like 'work' which makes it fun to do (and the passion tends to be contagious which will lend to your success as well).

Here are some important categories to consider when choosing a company.

1. Is the company going to last long term?

No one can be successful in a company that fails. Something to be aware of is that 95-98% of start-up companies fail and go out of business in the first 5 years. When researching a company, you may want to steer toward something that has proven to have staying power. If you find a start-up company that you just fall in love with it's fine to start a business there, I just want you to be aware of this statistic.

2. Does the product sell outside the network?

What I mean by this is to take a look at whether the company produces a product that people would buy even if there wasn't a business opportunity attached. Your best bet is to join a company with a valuable product that people will buy just for the sake of consuming the product (as a customer).

A valuable, consumable product is what produces residual income. When people fall in love with a product and continue to purchase it month after month, we then continue to get paid a commission on that consumer month after month (this is the definition of residual income).

A valuable product is the backbone of a successful company because it's what makes a consumer's life better. Only valuable products cause a consumer to keep purchasing them.

3. Will I be rewarded well for my efforts?

The answer to this question has to do with the compensation plan. You'll basically be doing the same amount of work regardless what company you decide to join, so you'll want to be sure the company you choose has a generous payout.

One of the most important aspects of a compensation plan, in my opinion, is the **residual payout**. This is the amount we get paid month after month that the consumer continues to purchase the product. If the company offers a strong residual payout, it makes it easy for us to build a strong residual income (money that comes in month after month regardless of whether we work or not). This is what creates time freedom.

If the compensation plan simply offers a generous 'fast start bonus' (a bonus that is received each time you refer a new member or customer) but not much in the way of a residual payout, this will mean that you will have to be continuously trading hours for dollars in order to be continuously getting paid. This type of income does not create time freedom.

4. What is the vision/intention of the company?

Good company intention is where the owners have a long-term vision of helping people with their products and a long-term vision of providing a valuable opportunity for their distributors. Good Network Marketing companies view their distributors as their greatest asset. You'll want to be sure that the company has a vision for the future and that they are poised for growth.

Here are some questions to ask when evaluating a company:

1. How did the company get started and who started it? Is the person/people who started it still involved? Has the company been sold to investors? If yes, it's not a good sign unless the purchaser has a similar or greater vision.

   You'll also want to ask some questions about the overall integrity of the company. One of the things I was impressed by about the company I decided to join is that they have never (in 26 years) had a backorder and the checks always get sent out on time and they always cash. This says a lot about the integrity of the company and this is a critical element to consider when looking at joining a company.

2. Is the company financially stable (capable of meeting financial obligations)? Is the company debt-free? One good way to find out the financial standing of a company is to check out their credit rating with Dunn & Bradstreet (a company that rates the credit and financial standing of businesses).

3. Is the company growing? Are this year's sales greater than last year? If not, it doesn't necessarily mean it's not a stable company, but if it's a growing company that's certainly a plus.

4. Does the company listen to and implement suggestions from leaders? The company doesn't necessarily have to implement all suggestions, but it's important that the people who are 'out in the field' (the distributors) are able to provide feedback and suggestions to the corporate offices of the company in order to create strategic plans and better products. Most good companies have some kind of 'leadership council' that is made up of some of the top leaders (distributors) in the company who get to have a say in the overall operation of the company.

5. If the company is over 10 years old, does it *reinvent* itself by opening new markets and creating new products? A "single" product company will most likely find itself running out of customers after a given period of time.

6. What kind of training is provided for new distributors? Because of the 'cooperative' structure of the Network Marketing business model, new distributors should be able to receive free training and ongoing coaching by other successful members of their company. You'll definitely want to make sure this type of training is in place before joining a company, as it's a lot less likely that you will be able to succeed completely on your own.

7. What's most important is to make your decision based on facts, so that you choose what is right for you. If you want to build a life by design, take action. And certainly don't let other people's opinions or outdated information determine your future. I'm happy that I took action when I did, and I know my children (once they're old enough to understand) will be happy that I did as well.

CHAPTER 9

MAKING A COMMITMENT

Your work is to discover your work and then, with all your heart, give yourself to it. ~ Buddha

A Network Marketing business is one that certainly demands effort. For some, it can be some of the hardest work we have ever done. However, if we stick with it, it has an approximate 3-5 year business plan instead of a 40-year one.

Many people quit in the early stages, as it sometimes feels like we are paid very little for our efforts. But those that stick it out long enough to see their success through are compensated extremely well (and have to put in much less effort than they did in the beginning).

One of the greatest things about this industry is that people are rewarded, and paid, according to the results that they achieve. It's one of the most ethical business models, and certainly one of the most fair.

You see, in the corporate world, people are paid according to their resumes, their education, their connections, and sometimes even their attractiveness. This, in my opinion, is unfair. In the Network Marketing industry, we get paid according to what we accomplish, and it's a level playing field. Those who produce the most get paid the most. It doesn't matter what kind of education you have or who you know at the top.

You Decide

When you join a Network Marketing company, you get to decide what kind of commitment you are going to make to your business. For some, it's 5-10 hours per week, and for others it may be 40 hours per week. You also get to choose what you'd like to accomplish and what your goals are. Some people simply want to create enough residual income to cover their mortgage payment, and others want to create $50,000 per month or more.

It's totally up to you, and it's all based on your commitment.

One of the pitfalls in our industry is that people join a company and expect to get rich overnight. This industry, in most cases, is not a get-rich-quick scheme. A Network Marketing business is something that's built steadily over time and creates a solid stream of residual income.

If residual income was something that could be created instantly, everyone would have it.

Creating residual income requires commitment.

The great thing about this industry and the commitment that's required, is that if you work your business consistently over time, you may be able to retire (and continue collecting your residual income month after month) after only 3-5 years. Although this may seem like a long time, it sure beats the 40-year retirement plan that comes along with most jobs.

Do Most People Fail at MLM?

You may have heard the claim, "Most people fail at MLM."

This statement actually cracks me up. First of all, it's usually made by the people who are trying to justify why they gave up or never got started.

Secondly, it's funny because the same thing can be said about pretty much anything else people attempt.

According to the National Association of Real Estate, over 80% of people who get their real estate license quit in their first year—most never sell one home.

Most people who want to play professional sports fail. Most people who start a business fail. Most people who want to play a musical instrument quit. Most people who want to get into shape quit. Most people who want to sing at the Opera fail.

If someone goes on a diet and exercise program and then cheats by eating things that are not on their diet program and/or by not exercising when they're supposed to, *can they really blame their "failure" on the diet and fitness industry?* Of course not.

If a person fails, it's simply because they gave up or they were not fully committed to begin with.

I'll Give It a Try

Some people join a Network Marketing company with the attitude, "I'll give it a try." Giving it a try is not the same thing as fully committing to it.

Here's the difference:

When someone is 'giving it a try', they will more than likely give up as soon as they hit a bump in the road.

When someone fully commits to succeeding with their business, they will keep pushing forward in the face of obstacles.

I can tell you that over the last 8 years that I've been in this industry, I've come up against a lot of people, including some of my closest friends and family members, who have told me that I would never succeed at this or that I was crazy for being involved. I know for a fact that if I wasn't fully committed to succeeding NO MATTER WHAT, that I probably would have given up a long time ago and followed the advice of the naysayers in my life.

I also know for a fact that, because of my commitment, I now have the lifestyle that many of those naysayers wish they had. And there lives now look identical (if not worse) than they did 8 years ago while my life has completely transformed for the better in all areas due to my commitment to my business.

Being 'Decided' Versus Being 'In the State of Deciding'

One of the ways to look at commitment is to ask yourself if you have 'decided' or if you are 'in the state of deciding'.

When you have 'decided', you have fully committed to doing this business and you are committed to succeeding no matter what (or who) you come up against.

When you are 'in the state of deciding' it basically means you are going to 'give this a try' and will most likely be done trying as soon as the going gets tough.

One really important distinction to understand about these 2 ways of being is that people are a lot less likely to want to join someone who is giving it a try. When you have decided and fully committed to your success, you'll find that people will be a lot more likely to want to join you and follow in your footsteps.

Carving Out Time

Everybody's lives are busy and, as a mother, I know how crazy our schedules can be.

One of the hugest pieces of the commitment when it comes to succeeding at a business like this is being able to carve out time in your already busy schedule to commit to building your business.

This might mean adjusting some of your priorities. You may have to spend an hour a day less with your spouse so that you can work on your business after your kids go to bed at night. Or you may need to spend your lunch hour making calls instead of socializing with co-workers.

Whatever the shift is that needs to be made, it all really comes down to being able to carve out, and commit to, the time to work our businesses. The fact of the matter is that this business is easy to do, but it's also really easy *not* to do. If we don't have the time carved out and scheduled, it's really easy to go through the day without making any time at all for our businesses.

Commitment is Key

Your commitment is a key factor to your success. Just like learning an instrument or wanting to play a professional sport, your business will probably not succeed without a strong commitment. The good news is that those who commit and fully decide that they're going to succeed in this industry usually do, and the payoff is huge and so worth it.

CHAPTER 10

FAMILY FUN

If one advances confidently in the direction of his dreams, and endeavors to live the life which he has imagined, he will meet with success unexpected in common hours. ~Henry David Thoreau

As a mother, what's great about this type of business is that we can do it with our kids in tow, and we can include them in our goals and celebrate our victories with them.

For example, in my business, we set goals for ourselves and we always put a reward in place for when we achieve the goal. The reward that I've put in place for when I achieve my next rank advancement is a trip to Disney World with my children (I will also be paying the way for the other mothers on my team who hit their goals, and their children, so that we can all celebrate together).

My kids are very excited about this trip. And at this point in my business I've gotten very good about creating clear boundaries as far as business time vs. family time. However, as a mother, sometimes the 2 worlds have to collide and I find myself needing to jump on a call or take care of business in some way while my kids are with me. When this happens, I simply mention that, "This is for Disney World." And I instantly have full cooperation from my kids.

They love to contribute to my success in any way they can. And they especially love that they get rewarded when I succeed (next time it's Disneyland, last year it was a beach house at the Jersey Shore).

CREATING A LIFE BY DESIGN

In the Network Marketing industry, we get to create a life by design. In other words, we get to decide what we'd like to have in our lives, and then we get to go out and create it.

In my company, we have a remarkable leadership retreat that happens every summer in the mountains in Colorado. We spend about a week together and get coached and trained on a very deep level. It's mostly "inner game" work, not training about the mechanics of doing the business, but training on personal growth topics such as having a vision, making a difference, etc.

Two summers ago, we were doing a session on vision and were asked to discover what we were going to have in our lives "no matter what". We were taught that when we find something that we're literally willing to go to the wall for, that absolutely nothing could stop us from being successful.

During this exercise, it hit me and tears started rolling down my face. Although I had many ideas about 'why' I was doing this business, I hadn't found anything that I was truly ready to have in my life "no matter what".

In that moment, I discovered it. I realized that it was completely unacceptable to me that my girls have no connection to my home state of New Jersey (my whole family lives in Colorado now so we don't go back to visit very frequently), and that they don't get to spend any time at the beach in the summer.

I grew up spending my summers at the Jersey Shore. My parents would rent a beach house on Long Beach Island every summer, a quaint little 15-mile-long island with white sand beaches, a little amusement park, and lots of great seafood restaurants and great Jersey pizza. I guess I took it for granted that I got to spend so much time near the ocean having been raised there.

Well, during this vision exercise, I realized that my kids had never experienced anything like this, and that they really have no idea what the place I grew up in was like whatsoever. I realized that this was unacceptable to me and that starting the following summer we were going to have a beach house on the Jersey shore during the summer, NO MATTER WHAT.

In that moment I became completely unstoppable in my business, and the following summer we had a beach house on Long Beach Island. My brother and his family (who also live in Colorado about 7 hours from us, so we don't get to see them nearly enough) joined us there, and so did my father. We got to enjoy time at the beach, the cousins (my kids and my brother's kids) got to have some serious quality time together, and my father got to be with all 4 of his grandkids.

This is what I mean when I talk about creating a life by design. You simply decide what you want, and you create it. The Network Marketing industry gives us the power to do this. And there is no limit to what you can create.

Building a Business with My Kids

The other awesome thing about this business is that we can actually build it while we're out frolicking with our kids.

When I'm out at a playground, the mall, the ice skating rink, etc. in the middle of the day, I meet other mothers. Most of these moms are stay-at-home moms who spend time with their kids while their husbands are off at work making money. When they find out that I'm a single mom and I'm the breadwinner, yet I'm hanging out at a playground in the middle of the 'work day', they want to know how that's possible. When I tell them that I have residual income (I usually have to explain what that means) and that I earned it by making a difference in the world, they usually want to know more. At that point, I simply schedule a time to do a business overview with them, and then we get back to playing.

Scheduling appointments like this is the gist of how we build our businesses, and we are able to do this while we're out playing with our kids. This is another perfect example of why the Network Marketing industry is such a perfect fit for mothers.

And, not only do we get to build our businesses while we're spending time with our children, but we get to make a profound difference and set an incredible example for other mothers while we're doing it.

CHAPTER 11

CINDY LAPP

www.BalanceYourBodyForLife.com

This business is a total no-brainer for moms. ~ Cindy Lapp

I've been in the Network Marketing industry for 4 years. Before I started in this industry I was the owner of several retail businesses. Now I do Network Marketing full-time and I have a 16-month-old grandson.

Thanks to the Network Marketing industry, I have an incredible amount of time freedom.

If I still owned my retail businesses, there's no way that I'd be able to spend the kind of time with my grandson that I'm spending with him now. For example, my grandson has been with me for the last 3 days. That was certainly not possible as a retail business owner. No way!

I'm able to weave my Network Marketing business around other commitments like being with my grandson, so my schedule is extremely flexible and can change from week to week.

My kids benefit as well. Being in this industry has allowed my children to completely have me. For example, my daughter knows that if something comes up there's a pretty good chance that she can rely on me to pinch hit for her, and I know that her and her husband would be up a creek without me. They love knowing that they can rely on us (my husband's in this business too), and that their son doesn't have to be shuffled from babysitter to babysitter.

This business is absolutely ideal for moms.

Being in the Network Marketing industry allows moms to choose how they want to spend their day, and when you have kids that's so incredibly important. A lot of moms have to miss a lot of their kids' lives, like activities at school or sporting events. This business allows moms to be able to participate in all of their children's activities and not have to miss any of it, because they get to work when they say. This business is a total no-brainer for moms.

This industry is also a good demonstration for kids.

This industry shows children that they get to create their own life, rather than being an employee. It just shows them that there are choices out there. I didn't know that growing up. I thought you had to go to school and get good grades so you can get a good job, or be chained to a retail business like I ended up doing.

I had no idea there were other choices. And I believe that this is the biggest gift you can give your kids. They may not choose this industry, but at least they'll know about it. And I bet that when they see the freedom that comes with it that they will choose it or something very similar. It's just a good education.

So many moms also lose their identity, especially when they choose to stay at home.

A lot of the time they have an idea that they then can't work outside the home, or they don't want to work outside the home. Sometimes being a mom, as fulfilling as it is, just isn't enough for a woman as her complete identity. So for a woman to be able to create her own business that doesn't take away from the family but actually contributes to the family in gigantic ways just makes a mom's life so much more fulfilling. This allows her to have something that she can create from the ground up. And there are just not many other opportunities for moms to do that and to be able to also stay home with their children.

CHAPTER 12

MAKING A DIFFERENCE

Act as if what you do makes a difference. It does. ~William James

Through this industry, I have been able to help a lot of people experience significant personal growth and improve their standard of living. To me, it's all about letting people know how much I care about them, whether they're simply using the products as customers, or joining me in my business. This industry truly provides an opportunity for all people to realize their dreams, and there's nothing I enjoy more than being a part of that.

MAKING A DIFFERENCE FOR OUR CHILDREN

The thing that I am, by far, the MOST passionate about when it comes to this business is that I get to, through my example, teach my children about the possibilities and options that exist for them. You see, our educational system is designed to teach our children to get good grades so that they can grow up and get a good job working for somebody else. That's what I was taught when I was a kid, and I grew up not even knowing that options like this even existed.

But now, by leading by example, I'm teaching my children that there's another way. I'm showing them that, even though I'm a single parent, I can still show up and have lunch at the school cafeteria with my daughter whenever I please, I can still chaperone field trips, and I never miss a beat in their lives. I'm showing them that I own my life, and teaching them that they, too, can own their lives when they grow up. I actually get choked up when I think about this because to me it is so utterly important. And I just love that I get to make this kind of a difference for my children.

Through this industry we have the capability to make a difference for our children in many other ways as well.

For example, my kids get to see me making a difference for people on a daily basis. They get to see me getting thanked by people whose lives have changed for the better because I shared a product or a service with them that has helped them to get their health back or to be financially free.

They also get to be a part of the incredible community that I have around me thanks to this business. They are, in turn, surrounded by success-minded people who are making a difference in the world (I know this has a huge impact on them because it's much different than the world I grew up in and I can only imagine what it would have been like to have been raised in a community like this).

Thanks to the personal growth that comes when we work in an industry such as Network Marketing, my children have also gotten to see me evolve into a leader. They've watched my life transform and my self-esteem increase over the years. I know that this certainly has a positive impact on them as well.

And they get to take great vacations and experience things that other kids might only dream about.

Most of all, they get to have their mom, present and available for them as they grow up.

MAKING A DIFFERENCE IN THE WORLD

Through the Network Marketing industry, we not only get to make a huge difference for our children, but we get to make a difference in the world as well.

The basic foundation of this industry is about making people's lives better. One of the greatest things about Network Marketing, in my opinion, is that **we have a unique opportunity to make a profound difference in the lives of others**. We are problem solvers, and we have so much to contribute.

If you want to TRULY succeed (in every sense of the word), the best way to do this is to approach your business consciously and come from a place of serving others.

We are problem solvers and we have the capacity and the opportunity to change lives for the better.

Think about it . . . if someone has a health issue (or would simply like more energy), there's a network marketer that can help them with that. If a person wishes that they had more time to spend with their children, there's a network marketer that can help them obtain that. If someone would like to have more money coming into their household, there's certainly a network marketer that can help solve that issue. Even if the 'problem' is something along the lines of needing to find some unique environmentally safe candles for a yoga studio, there's a network marketer that can assist with that. So many of the 'problems' people face in their lives (health, finances, time freedom, etc.) can be solved by the people in the Network Marketing industry.

As Zig Ziglar said,

> *"You can only get what you want, if you help enough other people get what they want."*

This is the foundation of our industry.

And if you care about every customer and member that you bring into your business as if they were your own children, you are bound to succeed here.

CHAPTER 13

RESIDUAL INCOME—WHY IT MATTERS FOR MOTHERS

Freedom is not something that anybody can be given. Freedom is something people take, and people are as free as they want to be. ~ *James Baldwin*

One of the biggest gifts that we get to enjoy when we have a business in the Network Marketing Industry is residual income.

Here's the definition I created that's also in the glossary of this book:

Residual Income: Income that continues to come in after you stop working. Often times in the Network Marketing industry, we do the work once and continue to get paid on it month after month, year after year. This income is generated due to the loyalty of our customers who continue to order products (usually through an automatic shipment that requires no extra work on the distributor's part) month after month. It is residual income that allows people in the Network Marketing industry to get paid whether they work or not, and it is this type of income that creates time freedom.

COMPANIES VARY

Something to keep in mind is that, depending on the company you join, the residual payout will vary. I highly recommend looking for a company with a generous residual payout.

If you join a company that has generous 'fast start' bonuses (bonuses that are paid out once at the time you enroll a new customer or member) but not a good residual payout, you will **not** be starting a business that is going to create walk-away residual income and time freedom because you will have to continue to work to receive the fast start bonuses. (This type of income is referred to as **linear income**—income where you get paid once on your efforts or income where you trade your hours for dollars. There is no time freedom when you are working for linear income.)

True wealth in the Network Marketing industry comes from the creation of residual income.

MY RELATIONSHIP TO RESIDUAL INCOME AND WHY I'M SO PASSIONATE ABOUT IT

I have always been passionate about creating residual income and the time freedom and lifestyle freedom that it has the power to provide for people.

However, due to some circumstances that I have experienced in my own life, my level of passion about residual income has increased significantly, and I've realized that part of my purpose while I'm alive is to show others that this is a possibility for them as well.

I am particularly passionate about sharing this message with mothers. I truly believe that every mother and all families should experience the type of financial security that is available when one earns residual income. I also believe that all parents should have time freedom so that they can enjoy their children on a daily basis. Residual income provides this time freedom.

SHARING YOUR GIFTS

I also know that many mothers tend to lose their sense of identity and are not always connected to their gifts that the world is waiting for them to share. As women and as mothers, we often get so wrapped up in our roles as mothers and wives that we don't allow ourselves to pursue our true passions and share our gifts.

Many women actually have guilt around pursuing the things that they're passionate about because they feel that doing so would take time and energy away from their children and their families.

I believe the opposite. I know that my children grow and expand as they watch me grow, live my true passions, and make a difference in the world. It provides something for them and, through my example, I give my children permission to live into their true gifts as well.

Besides the guilt that I mentioned, some other things that often get in the way of women following their passion are financial constraints and time constraints. Residual income relieves both of these issues. Once there is financial abundance due to residual income, true time freedom is created and mothers are then freed up to focus on their dreams and passions.

TRUE TIME FREEDOM

I love that when I wake up in the morning, I know that I'm getting paid whether I choose to work that day or not. I love that I can take my kids to the pool, enjoy myself, be fully present, and relax knowing that the check will be coming in the mail regardless.

A more extreme example is when I went through my divorce with a 4-week-old and a 3-year-old and had to take 4 months away from my business to handle moving, lawyers, therapy, etc. and I got paid the entire time. I didn't have to go out and get a job like most single mothers would have, and I was extremely grateful for this during a traumatic time when my children really needed me to be there for them.

It was actually this experience that helped me to realize what a true gift residual income is. It was this experience (as difficult as it was) that led me to my true purpose, to show other mothers that this type of security is available for them as well.

FINANCIAL SECURITY

I'm certainly aware that every mother is not going to end up going through a divorce. But the fact of the matter is that life is uncertain, and I do know that many women would be in a delicate situation if suddenly their husband's income was removed from the picture. Having a stream of residual income would save the day in a situation like this. I know this for certain from first-hand experience.

And, even when there is not an extreme circumstance like this, residual income simply provides a type of financial security that would benefit all families.

I absolutely love knowing that my income is secure. There are many people today who certainly cannot say that they have secure income, especially with the fragility and uncertainty of today's job market. Wouldn't it be nice to wake up every morning knowing that your family's financial future is secure?

As a mother, knowing that my children completely depend on me every single day, I can't imagine having it any other way.

NEVER MISS A BEAT

The thing about residual income and what it provides for me as a single mother that is nearest and dearest to my heart is the fact that, because of the time freedom it gives me in my life, I never have to miss a beat in my children's lives.

I love that I can chaperone my daughter's field trips in the middle of the day, or show up and participate in her classroom. I get to attend all of her 'spring sings', field days, and school functions.

Being able to actively participate in my children's lives on a daily basis is priceless to me. If you are a parent, you know how fast these childhood moments fly by and we will never get them back.

And, because of this, I will be forever grateful for residual income and forever passionate about helping other parents to have it.

When you have brought up kids, there are memories you store directly in your tear ducts. ~Robert Brault

CHAPTER 14

ALI ALVAREZ

www.PhoneOnFire.com

One day you wake up and you have built a whole new life of freedom for yourself and your family. ~ Ali Alvarez

My name is Ali and I am the mother of two small children.

I have been a yoga teacher for 10 years, and when I had my first child, I didn't want to return to the long hours away from home. I live just outside of New York City, and the high cost of childcare was prohibitive. I didn't want to pay someone else to raise my children. I wanted to raise my children. I wanted to be there every step of the way with them.

So I was in fact searching for an MLM company without realizing I was searching for an MLM company.

Then entered my exuberant neighbor who followed me around for several days inviting me to check out what he was doing, and he thought it would be a good fit for me. I said, "NO". I knew it was Network Marketing, and although I was not one of those skeptics that says "Oh it's a pyramid scheme", I just didn't know anything about the industry, nor did I know anyone who actually made any money in the industry. I didn't even realize that my past dabbling in cosmetics was in fact Network Marketing.

"I'm too busy." I said to my neighbor. And he, being persistent, didn't give up on me. A week went by of blissful silence.

I said no to MLM, but MLM didn't say no to me.

I was doing laundry in the basement when my neighbor came in with the mail. "Hey, Ali, got a minute? Can I show you something?"

"Sure."

"Well," he exclaims as he rips open his mail, "Here is my monthly check from an MLM company that I worked for over 10 years ago. I haven't done a thing with this company for 10 years and I still get paid every month." He handed me his check for $250 and I flipped my banana. In that moment I finally understood. I looked him square in the eyes and said, "Let's talk."

So began my journey deep and strong into this strange and highly misunderstood world of MLM. I started to read everything I could get my hands on about this business and industry. As my understanding deepened so did my passion for what I now hold.

The way I see it is this. Someone invites you to climb a mountain. And you have a choice. You can say, "No thanks, I like it here on the ground very much and wouldn't want to change anything about my life." Or you can look this opportunity in the eyes and say "Yes! Lets' do it, let's climb."

So those who say "No" stay outside where it is safe and nothing changes and those who say "Yes" walk inside.

Inside is a big world, a very big world. There are lots of amazing guides who have climbed before you who are going to help you on your journey. These guides have either reached the mountain's summit, or they are further on the path to getting there.

There are lots of tools here on the inside. There are different kinds of tools for different approaches up your mountain. They all work, you just have to decide which tools you are going to use for your particular trek up.

It's not a short and quick path, it can be a long and challenging road, but each tier you climb you can look behind you and see the distance you covered, and the growth you have accomplished.

I've burned the bridge behind me. For me, there is no going back.

I know what I want to create with my life, I can see it, and I am dedicated to this process for getting me there.

It's not for everyone, just like being an employee is not for everyone. Being an employee is safe and comfortable. But when you are an employee you are building for someone else. This is building for me and my family, and what is truly incredible is the amount of resources and support that are out there to help me create my business.

As a mother who works from home, it's like a neat little iPad that pops out when my kids nap, or comes along with me to the playground. It's funny that sometimes I find great challenges in carving out my business hours around the unpredictability of life and children, and there are other moments when I've put my business away for a day when someone finds me who is interested in what I am doing, and what I have to offer so my little business window opens once more.

That is how this builds, person by person, brick by brick, and one day you wake up and you have built a whole new life of freedom for yourself and your family.

CHAPTER 15

LEAVING A LEGACY

The legacy of heroes is the memory of a great name and the inheritance of a great example. ~ *Benjamin Disraeli*

Last but certainly not least, I want to address the fact that this industry provides us with a vehicle to leave a legacy, for our children and future generations.

We've talked about residual income and how we get to create this type of income (that continues to come in even after we stop working) in the Network Marketing industry.

We've discussed how residual income is a phenomenal way to fund your retirement, allowing you to be able to travel and live large after you've completely stopped working.

Now let's talk about leaving a legacy.

One of the most incredible things that industry provides is a way for us to create a stream of income that we can actually will to our children or to the foundation of our choice upon our own death. So the income doesn't stop coming in *even after we die*. Is that amazing or what?

So, although we have to put in some elbow grease in the beginning to create our residual income (and, again, this is not a get-rich-quick scheme), isn't it worth it to know that that income stream will continue to come in and support our families or the causes that we believe in even after we're gone?

Also, think about the other type of legacy you will leave. By making a difference in the world and being the family breadwinner, you are instilling incredible traits and values into your children that they will be able to pass on to their children and the rest of the future generations. This piece is invaluable and gives me reason enough to want to be a part of this incredible industry.

One of the things that I reflect upon daily as I go through my days is, "What kind of legacy am I leaving? What kind of impression am I making on my children? How will they remember me, and speak about me, when I'm gone?"

I know that by being present in their lives, being the family breadwinner, making a difference in the lives of others, providing an abundant lifestyle for them, and developing myself into a leader, I am leaving my legacy.

And I have to say I literally owe it all to the Network Marketing industry. I seriously don't even recognize myself or my life from the way it was 8 years ago. And I'm glad my children didn't know me then.

CHAPTER 16

CONCLUSION

Remember, Ginger Rogers did everything Fred Astaire did, but backwards and in high heels. ~Faith Whittlesey

Have you ever heard the Dalai Lama talk about how the saving of the world will be left up to the Western woman?

Women are way more powerful than we even begin to give ourselves credit for. We have so many wonderful innate qualities, many of which are typically under-utilized.

Simply mothering a child in and of itself requires a great deal of power. If you think about it, there are virtually no limits to what we can do when we set our minds to it.

The Network Marketing industry, thanks to the financial freedom and the time freedom that it provides, is an ideal vehicle that women and mothers can tap into so that we can free ourselves up to make an enormous difference in the world.

So I urge you take advantage of this incredible vehicle. Start now. The world deserves your gifts, and so do your children.

The thing women have yet to learn is nobody gives you power. You just take it. ~Roseanne Barr

ABOUT THE AUTHOR

Amy Starr Allen is a single mom, and she is a fine example of the emerging class of mompreneurs; stay-at-home mothers achieving financial success while raising wonderful children. Amy is passionate about helping to make it possible for mothers to stay with their children and still be bread-winners.

Amy is the founder of *Moms Empowering Moms,* an organization that she created as a resource for mothers to support and empower each other to become leaders within their families, communities, businesses, and lives.

Amy is also an author, a business trainer and coach, a singer-songwriter, and the owner of a successful Network Marketing business. She is committed to helping people create financial freedom and time freedom (more time with their families) in their lives through the power of residual income.

Amy believes that moms are better role models when they're pursuing something they're passionate about and teaching their children that they can be their own boss. Her foundation is based on the idea that you can be a great mother and still make a difference in other people's lives.

Growing up as a gymnast, Amy has been passionate about fitness since she was a young child, and finds her purpose in making a difference for people in regards to self-esteem, awareness, and well-being. She has always encompassed the entrepreneurial spirit and holds several professional certifications. She has worked in real estate, she is a certified personal trainer with a background in health, nutrition, fitness, and wellness, and she has a specialty certification in pre & post-natal fitness. Much of her work has been devoted to helping women during their childbearing years before, during, and after pregnancy to obtain and maintain optimal health and fitness. She is also a labor and postpartum doula and has worked to support women in their transitions to motherhood by providing emotional, physical, informational, and practical support. She is a member of the Colorado Doulas Association and the Holistic Moms Network.

Amy makes her home in Boulder, Colorado with her 2 daughters, Olivia and Ava.

RESOURCES

Amy Starr Allen can be contacted via her website at www.AmyStarrAllen.com.

Moms Empowering Moms is an organization that supports financial awakening, profound community, and leadership development for mothers. You can learn more about Moms Empowering Moms at www.MomsEmpoweringMoms.com.

Nicole S. Cooper can be contacted via her website at www.TheMailboxMoneyBlog.com

Chante Epps-McDonald can be contacted via her website at www.ChanteEpps.com.

Cindy Lapp can be contacted via her website at www.BalanceYourBodyForLife.com.

Ali Alvarez can be contacted via her website at www.PhoneOnFire.com.